PLENTY
OF PATCHES

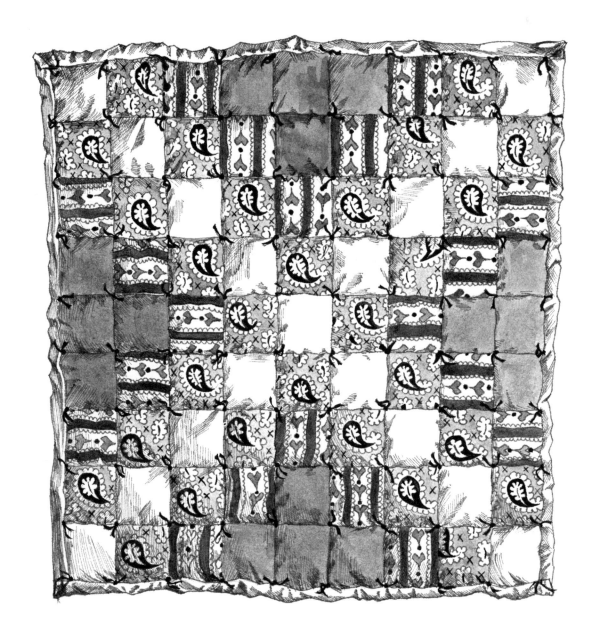

MARILYN RATNER

PLENTY
OF PATCHES

An Introduction to Patchwork,
Quilting, and Appliqué

illustrated by Chris Conover

Thomas Y. Crowell   New York

*This book
is dedicated to
Michael, David,
and Jo.*

Library of Congress Cataloging in Publication Data
Ratner, Marilyn. Plenty of patches.
Includes index.
SUMMARY: Instructions for creating various items using quilting, patchwork, and appliqué.
1. Patchwork—Juv. lit.   2. Quilting—Juv. lit.   3. Appliqué—Juv. lit.
[1. Patchwork.   2. Quilting.   3. Appliqué.   4. Handicraft]   I. Conover, Chris.   II. Title.
TT835.R35   746.4'6   77-3401   ISBN 0-690-01329-9   0-690-03836-4 (LB)

10 9 8 7 6 5 4 3 2 1

CONTENTS

INTRODUCTION

Add a perky patchwork pocket to your favorite pair of jeans; dress up your room with a bold checkerboard quilt; turn an ordinary bookbag into a work of art with a colorful patchwork design.

These are only a few of the projects you can make with this book. All are designed to achieve striking effects with a minimum amount of sewing. If you're a beginner, everything you need to know about tools and materials and sewing techniques is explained in the beginning sections, so please read these before starting on your first project.

To make sure your sewing efforts are successful, each project has very detailed instructions and drawings to guide you from start to finish. There is no reason why you can't soon make a quilt that will become a family heirloom, but it's best to start with something simple, such as a pillow or potholder. These are a good introduction to projects requiring more time and patience.

To help you choose projects suited to your skill, each one has a code. One-patch projects are the easiest. Two-patch projects require more planning and sewing. Three-patch projects are the most challenging.

One of the exciting things about today's patchwork is that there are so many gorgeous fabrics to work with. Depending on the colors and patterns you select for a project, you can achieve a bold look, a subdued look, an old-fashioned look, or a modern look. So even though exact directions are given for each project, the choice of fabric pattern and of color is left to each sewer. You aren't told to put a red patch next to a blue one. This way, each patchwork is your special creation.

Patchwork is often confused with quilting but actually it's one form of the craft. A quilt is a fabric sandwich made of a top, a bottom or backing, and a soft filler in between. A quilt top can be patchwork, which is pieces of fabric sewn together to form a larger piece of fabric, or it can be a single piece of fabric. Quilting is the process of joining the layers of a quilt together with lines of small stitches.

You will learn how to quilt when making some of the projects, and you also learn appliqué, the technique of sewing fabric cutouts to a background fabric. Once you've experimented with patchwork, quilting, and appliqué, you can mix them in projects you design yourself.

While quilting is an ancient craft, dating back to the Chinese and Egyptians who wore quilted clothing for warmth, patchwork is peculiarly American. It was born out of necessity early in American history when the quilts that the colonists brought from Europe wore out. Cloth was scarce in the new country, so women stitched scraps of fabric over the worn spots. This "patch work" was very simple at first. When fabric became easier to obtain in the middle of the eighteenth century, women fashioned quilts that showed off a wide assortment of fabrics and colors. Hundreds and sometimes thousands of geometric shapes were used to form striking patterns such as stars, crosses, and checkerboards. Patchwork was used for other articles besides bedcoverings—flags, tablecloths, and even clothing. Then, as now, the craft resulted in things that were beautiful as well as practical. Now, as then, it's a craft that allows anyone to be an artist. Here's to a bright beginning!

PLENTY
OF PATCHES

WHAT YOU NEED

One of the nice things about patchwork is that you don't need a lot of equipment and what you do need is not all that expensive. The basic supplies are a needle and thread, pins, a ruler, sharp scissors, quilt batting, and, of course, fabric. The equipment can be purchased in department stores, sewing-supply stores, and variety stores. If you already sew or know someone who does, then you may have enough scraps of material available for your first few projects. Otherwise, you will have to buy fabric. Left-over fabric can start your scrap collection. In fact, the patchwork String Tote, described later in the book, makes an elegant scrap bag. To accumulate scraps of fabric for future projects, ask friends and relatives who sew for leftovers. Also check remnant tables in stores. That's where odd-sized pieces of fabric are sold, usually for less than the regular price.

Supplies

When you go shopping for supplies, here's what to look for:

Needles. Use all-purpose sewing needles. Buy a package of assorted sizes so that you can find a needle that feels comfortable. For hand-quilting, use a short, sharp needle, #8 or #9. This type of needle makes it easy to stitch through three layers of material.

Thread. Any sewing thread is acceptable, but if possible use mercerized cotton or cotton-wrapped polyester thread. (These descriptions should be marked on the spool.) They are less likely to knot and twist. White or off-white thread is all you need for joining patches and ordinary sewing. Use colored thread for basting, because the stitches are easier to see.

Pins. Medium-sized straight pins do the job. The kind with a plastic or glass head are easiest to see. Use a pincushion to keep track of pins.

Thimble. A thimble is not really necessary for ordinary sewing, but for hand-quilting it is. You need one that fits your middle finger.

Pencil. A medium lead pencil is good for marking fabric. If the fabric is a dark color, use a light-colored artist's pencil. Tailor's chalk is not as good as pencil because it smudges.

Cardboard. Smooth, stiff cardboard—not the corrugated kind—is good for making templates.

Heavy Brown Paper. This is the kind of paper used for grocery bags or for mailing packages. It's easy to keep track of patches if you pin them to paper before sewing. Shelving paper is a substitute. Sometimes you need to tape a few sheets together to have a large enough piece.

Tracing Paper. Some projects call for tracing paper, which is used to trace patterns for templates.

Scissors. Household scissors are good for cutting cardboard templates. For cutting fabric, it's best to use dressmaker's scissors. Fabric scissors shouldn't be used to cut paper because paper dulls the blades.

Ruler. An ordinary ruler is fine for measuring fabric, drafting templates, and various measuring jobs. It can also be used to mark seam lines, but a sewing guide is easier if you have one.

Seam Ripper. This tool is not absolutely necessary, but it's a great help in removing mistakes, which are bound to occur.

Sewing Machine. All the projects in this book can be sewn by hand, but if you have a sewing machine and want to use it, fine. Make sure it is in good repair.

Iron. You will have seams to press, so you need an iron in proper working order. Always press on the wrong side of the fabric.

Fabric Facts

The most important thing to remember about fabric for quilting is that the fabric must suit the project. A sturdy cotton is perfect for a book bag, for example, while delicate satins or velvets are impractical. Cotton and cotton blends are recommended for all the projects in this book because they are easy to sew, wash well, and wear well. Especially if you are a beginner, don't choose hard-to-manage fabrics like flimsy organdy or heavy brocade. Knit fabrics are great for clothes, but they can stretch, so they should be avoided. Once you've had some experience, you may want to try working with unusual fabrics, but at first stick to such fabrics as calico, gingham, muslin, percale, chintz, polished cotton, and any of the cotton blends. It's fine to use fabric scraps—and patchwork encourages it—but fabric should be easy to manage and in good condition.

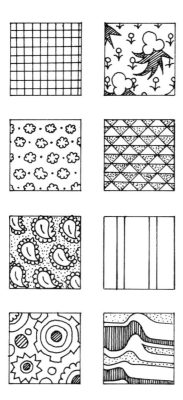

When deciding which material to buy or use, think of the weight of the fabric. If it's practical for a shirt or summer dress, it's probably fine for quilting. If it's fabric for a winter jacket or bathrobe, it's too heavy. The fabrics for a project should all be of the same weight.

Some projects encourage you to recycle jeans or an old shirt for patches. If you do use old clothes, remember to use the good parts, not the worn parts, or your project will be worn before you begin.

Shopping for Fabric

If you are buying fabric instead of using scraps, here are some guidelines to help you choose. Good-quality cotton is the best choice, but 100 percent cotton is hard to find. Cotton blends are made of cotton plus dacron, rayon, or another material. When buying blends, try to get the highest percentage of cotton possible. Look at the writing on the end of the bolt (fabric is usually folded and wrapped around a length of heavy cardboard), to see the fabric's contents. The label also tells how wide the fabric is. Cotton and cotton blends are usually 45 or 60 inches wide. Smaller projects call for less than ¼ yard of each fabric, but it's a good idea to buy more fabric than you need. Then, if you change your mind about the patchwork design or make a mistake, you won't have to run back to the store for more fabric. Extra fabric can always be used for another project. Ask salespeople questions about the fabric if you're unsure.

A good way to learn about fabric is by feeling it. Hold a small amount between your fingers and think about its weight, weave, and texture. Think how you'll use the fabric. Will it get a lot of wear and tear or just be decorative?

As you wander through the fabric selection, have an idea of which colors you want. Do you like red, yellow, and blue? Then choose a print with these colors. Look for another print with the same colors or a solid fabric to go with it. Be adventurous. Stripes, checks, florals, and prints can be used for the same project if *you* like the combination. Before making a final decision, place the fabrics next to each other and imagine how they will look cut into small patches. A big print may look great on the bolt but not as a 2-inch-square patch. If you simply can't make up your mind, buy a few more fabrics than the project calls for. You can always use leftover fabric. After all, the fun of patchwork is the effect of different fabrics used together. Sometimes this is hard to see until you are actually working on a project.

Batting

Quilt batting is sold in large rolls to fit different-sized beds. It's available in sewing-supply stores, variety stores, and in some department stores. Polyester batting is recommended. If you plan to make a bedcover, buy a large roll and use leftover batting for smaller projects. If you need only a small piece and don't want to buy batting, flannel is a good substitute.

Quilting Terms

All the quilting terms you need to know are in a section at the back of the book, "Terms to Know." Refer to it if you come across a word you aren't sure of. If you've done any sewing, you probably know many of these terms already.

4

HOW-TOS FOR ALL PROJECTS

Making Templates

Templates are cardboard patterns used to outline the patches on the fabric. The template is placed on the wrong side of the fabric and outlined with a sharp pencil. Then it's moved and traced again until all the patches are drawn. There are two kinds of templates: solid and window.

A solid template is the easiest to make. Simply draw the shape on a stiff piece of cardboard. The template is the size of the finished patch plus the seam allowance. So a 6-inch-square template is needed if the finished patches are 5 inches square and the seam allowance is $1/2$ inch. Cut out the template with a sharp pair of scissors, making sure that the corners are sharp and the edges are cleanly cut.

A window template is made the same way, only the center is also cut out, leaving a see-through piece of cardboard defining the cutting line and the seam line. The nice thing about a window template is that when you outline the patch on the fabric, you can draw the seam line at the same time. With a solid template, seam lines are drawn after the patches are cut.

To help you make both kinds of templates accurately, full-sized patterns are given for the first few projects. Trace the pattern on a sheet of tracing paper, glue the tracing paper to cardboard, then cut the cardboard to size.

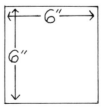 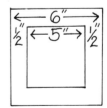

Finding the Straight Grain of the Fabric

It's good practice to cut patches on the straight grain of the fabric so that your project will hold its shape better, especially if it will be washed. The grain has to do with how the fabric is woven. The narrow woven border on the lengthwise edge of fabric is the selvage. Those threads running parallel to the selvage are the lengthwise or straight grain. Those threads running from selvage to selvage are the crosswise grain. The bias is a line diagonal to the grain.

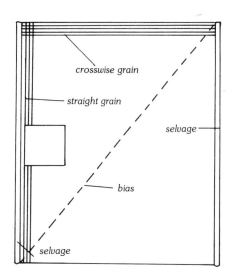

Sometimes fabric is "off grain" and has to be squared off. To test the fabric, straighten an end by cutting straight across the fabric. Next, fold the fabric in half lengthwise, matching the selvages. If the grains cross at right angles, the fabric is fine. If not, pull the fabric on the bias until the threads are straight.

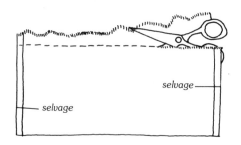

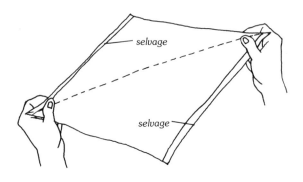

Cutting Patches

In addition to placing templates on the straight grain, you may want to position them so that patches show a particular part of the fabric's design. If so, it's best to use a window template so you can see exactly which part of the pattern will show. In general, the fabric should run the same way in as many patches as possible.

If you have several patches to cut from the same fabric, you may want to cut more than one at a time. Don't take this shortcut unless you're an experienced sewer. It's hard to keep the fabric from shifting, and patches may not come out the same size.

Marking Seam Lines

The seam line is marked on the wrong side of each fabric patch. It shows you where to stitch. For most projects, the seam allowance is $1/2$ inch. Use a ruler or sewing guide to measure the seam allowance. If you use a solid template, mark seam lines after cutting the patches. Work on a flat surface so that patches don't shift. If you use a window template, seam lines are marked at the same time the patch is outlined.

To mark seam lines, measure $1/2$ inch in from the edge in two or three places. Draw short lines for each marking. Then connect the short lines for a continuous line. Repeat on all sides of the patch.

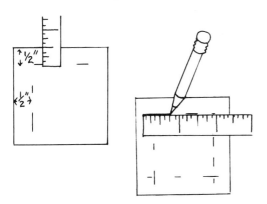

Joining Patches

Sewing patches together is often called *piecing*. Patches are always pieced the same way. Place two patches with right sides of the fabric facing. Pin them together along the seam line. Baste close to the seam line with large running stitches. Remove the pins. Stitch with a running stitch if hand-sewing, or a straight stitch if machine-sewing. Remove basting.

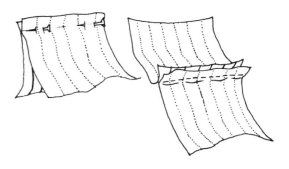

Continue joining patches in this way until you have the right-sized patchwork called for in the project. (To keep you from getting mixed up, directions for each project suggest an order for sewing patches.) Press seams after sewing each one, so that your work is always smooth and flat. Press seams to one side, on the wrong side of the fabric.

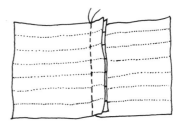

Sewing

Any of the projects can be sewn by hand or with a sewing machine. Each method has its advantages, but the one you decide to use really depends on how you like to sew. Hand-sewing is portable. You can piece patches while visiting a friend or watching TV or taking a car trip. Machine-sewing is faster, and the seams will probably be sturdier, depending on your skill with the machine.

Whichever way you sew, use white or off-white thread for joining patches. It's too much trouble to keep changing thread to go with different-color fabrics.

Stitches For Hand-Sewing:

Running Stitch. This is the main stitch used for sewing seams. Weave the needle in and out of the material, making evenly spaced stitches. Take only a few stitches at a time. You can start and end each seam with a knot or backstitch.

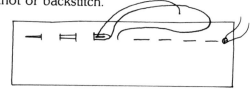

Basting. Long running stitches that temporarily hold pieces of fabric together.

Backstitch. This is a running stitch going backward. Bring the needle through the material and take a small stitch backward, close to where the last stitch was taken. For a strong seam, backstitch for a few stitches at the beginning and the end.

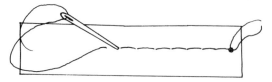

Slipstitch. This is a hemming stitch, and it's also used for appliqué. Take a stitch through the under fabric into the fold. Then take a stitch from the fold diagonally to the under fabric. Catch only a little of the under fabric and the fold. Come up a short distance away for the next stitch. The small, slanting stitches should be evenly spaced.

Blind Stitch. This is another hemming stitch for sewing borders, for appliqué, and for times when you don't want stitches to show. Bring the needle up from the under fabric through the fold. Take a stitch back through the under fabric at right angles (perpendicular) to the fold. Move the needle diagonally

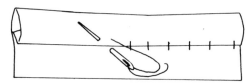

and come up through the fold a short distance away for the next stitch.

Whipstitch. This is an evenly spaced overcast stitch to join two pieces of fabric. Bring the needle from the back to the front, then up and over the edge of the fabric and from the back to the front again. Take each stitch slightly to the left of the one before it.

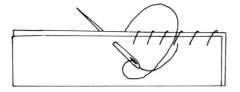

Stitches For Machine-Sewing:

Straight Stitch. A continuous row of running stitches.

Zigzag Stitch. The needle moves from side to side, making stitches that look like z's.

Satin Stitch. A closely spaced zigzag stitch used for appliqué and decorative sewing.

Estimating Yardage

For a large project such as a bed quilt, you need to figure the amount of fabric before going shopping. An easy way is to take the size of the template and figure how many patches will fit across a width of fabric. For example, if the fabric is 45 inches wide and the template is 10 inches square, you can cut four patches from a width. So, from a yard of fabric you can cut twelve patches. Don't count on using every inch of fabric.

1. Nine-Patch Pillow

Plan a pillow of just nine patches. Make them squares of equal size. This is the easiest kind of patchwork. Patchwork *can* be made with very small and varied shapes, but it doesn't have to be. Remember early quiltmakers spent the long, cold winter sewing tiny patches together. This pillow can be completed in one or two afternoons.

Think of the pillow front as a puzzle. Puzzle pieces are patches cut from different fabrics. The challenge: to fit pieces together in an eye-catching way. You should arrange the patches first one way, then another until you decide which way they look best.

The process for making any patchwork article is always the same, so the directions given here are useful for all the projects in this book and any you yourself might design later on. Don't skip any steps at first. Each one helps the puzzle to fit at the end. If you aren't sure of a step, look back at "How-tos for All Projects."

The finished pillow is 12 inches square. The patchwork front has three rows of three patches each. Each patch is 4 inches square when finished, but patches are cut 5 inches square to include the seam allowance, which is $1/2$ inch.

Choose three fabrics you like. You can use more—each patch can be different—but remember that all the fabrics should be of the same weight. Use a print and two solids, two prints and one solid, three stripes. Do the fabrics harmonize? You be the judge.

What You Need

Supplies. A pencil, a sheet of tracing paper, scissors, glue, a ruler, a 5-inch-square piece of heavy cardboard, a 12-inch-square piece of heavy brown paper, pins, a needle, white thread, colored thread for basting, and an iron.

Materials. Three or more fabrics—less than ¼ yard of each. Medium-weight cotton and cotton blends are suggested as they are easiest to handle. If you buy fabric, don't worry about buying more than you need—leftover fabric can be used for another project. You need a 13-inch-square piece of fabric for the pillow backing, and a 12-inch-square knife-edge pillow form or a bag of polyester pillow stuffing for filling.

How to Make

1. Make a cardboard template. Trace the pattern shown in the drawing on page 13 on a sheet of tracing paper. Glue it to a piece of cardboard and cut to size (5 inches square). Or simply measure and cut a 5-inch-square piece of cardboard.

2. Lay the template on the wrong side of the fabric and trace around it with a sharp pencil. You need nine patches. You could

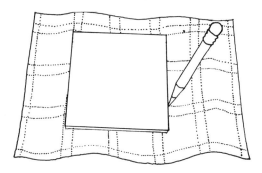

make three patches of each fabric and arrange them so that no two like patches touch, or use three patches of one fabric, four of another, and two of another. If you aren't sure of the design you want, cut a few extra patches of each fabric. Then you can try different arrangements.

3. Cut out all the patches. Cut carefully because the patches must all be the same size if they are to fit together properly.

4. Draw the seam lines ½ inch from the edges.

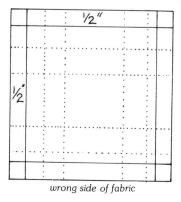

wrong side of fabric

5. Cut a 12-inch-square piece of heavy brown paper and lay it on a flat surface—the floor is a good place to work. Arrange the patches in three rows. When you have ordered them the best way, pin each patch to the paper, overlapping the patches by ½ inch. Now if you have to stop work, you can put everything away and the patches are in place on the paper until you have time to continue working.

6. At last, you're ready to sew. The num-

This pattern can be traced and used for the template.

13

bered sketch suggests an easy order for sewing patches together.

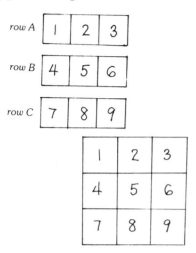

Unpin patches 1 and 2 from the brown paper. With right sides facing, pin them together along the seam line. Baste, then remove pins.* Stitch with a running stitch. Remove basting. Press the seams to one side.†

7. Join patches 2 and 3 the same way. Press. Join patches 4 and 5, and patches 5 and 6. Press. Join patches 7 and 8, and patches 8 and 9. Press.

8. Now join rows A and B. Pin and baste the two rows together, right sides facing. This means that patches 1 and 4 face, patches 2 and 5 face, and patches 3 and 6 face. Stitch, then press.

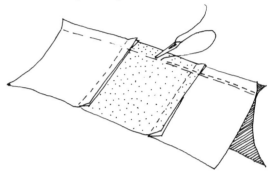

9. Join rows B and C the same way. Press. The pillow front is finished. If this were a bedcover, you would place a layer of batting between the top and backing for warmth, but since the pillow is decorative, it's finished like a pillow case.

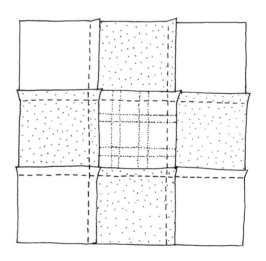

10. Cut the backing fabric 13 inches square. Draw seam lines ¹/₂ inch from the edges (always mark the wrong side of the fabric).

11. Pin the backing and patchwork together, right sides facing. Baste, close to the seam lines, on three sides. Leave the bottom seam open.

12. Stitch around three sides. Remove basting.

13. Fold the raw edges of the unfinished seam toward the wrong side and baste.

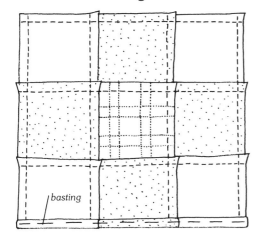

basting

14. Turn the work right side out. Insert a 12-inch pillow form or pillow stuffing.††

15. Slipstitch (see page 8) the opening closed. Remove basting. Perch the pillow on your favorite chair or on the bed.

Pointers

Basting keeps the fabric from shifting and means you can work without constantly sticking yourself with pins. Baste with a contrasting color thread so that stitches are easy to remove.

† Always press patchwork seams to one side instead of pressing them flat and open. Press toward the darker fabric if possible. Then seams won't show through.

†† Using a pillow form the same size means the pillow will look nice and plump, but it also means you have to struggle to get the pillow form inside the patchwork case. If you use pillow stuffing, stuff generously so that the pillow is firm.

Variations

If you're really ambitious, the other side of the pillow can be a totally different nine-patch design. Or make a floor pillow 24 inches square by fitting together four nine-patch blocks for the pillow front. The back can be a solid fabric, preferably a dark color so that it won't show dirt.

2. Quilted Potholder

SKILL

Any cook on your gift list will be delighted to receive this quilted potholder. It's a simple four-patch design, so you can make it in an afternoon. The finished patches are 4 inches square. Use the actual-size pattern for the Nine-Patch Pillow in the previous project to make a template.

The potholder combines patchwork and quilting techniques and gives you a chance to practice smooth sewing. Very little fabric is required, so use scraps from other sewing projects if you have them.

What You Need

Supplies. A pencil, a sheet of tracing paper, glue, a 5-inch-square piece of heavy cardboard, scissors, a ruler, pins, a needle, white thread, colored thread for basting, a #8 or #9 short needle for quilting, and an iron.

Materials. For the four patches, you need small amounts of at least two fabrics (you could also make each patch from a different fabric). Medium-weight cotton and cotton blends are easiest to handle. The backing is an 8½-inch square of medium-weight cotton. It can be one of the fabrics used for patches. For the filler, you need an 8½-inch-square piece of quilt batting or a piece of an old mattress pad or several layers of flannel. You need a package of 1-inch-wide bias tape to bind the edges. The tape should be one of the colors in the patchwork.

How to Make

1. Make a 5-inch-square cardboard template by tracing the pattern for the Nine-Patch Pillow on a sheet of tracing paper. Glue it to a piece of cardboard and cut to

size. Or simply measure and cut a 5-inch-square piece of cardboard.

2. Lay the template on the wrong side of each fabric and outline the patches. If using two fabrics, trace two patches from each.

3. Cut out the patches and mark seam lines $1/2$ inch from the edges.

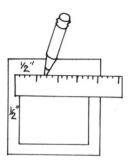

4. To join patches 1 and 2, first pin them together along the seam line with right sides facing. Baste, then remove pins and stitch. Remove basting. Press the seams to one side.

5. Join patches 3 and 4 the same way. Then join the two sections. Press the seams to one side.

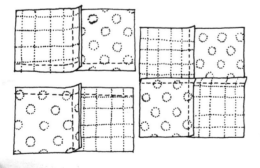

6. Trim the patchwork $1/4$ inch all around.

7. Cut the backing and batting to size ($8 1/2$ inches square).

8. On the right side of the patchwork, lightly pencil lines for quilting lengthwise, crosswise, and from corner to corner.

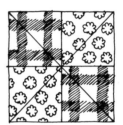

9. Lay the backing face down. Position the batting on top and lay the patchwork on top of the batting, right side up.

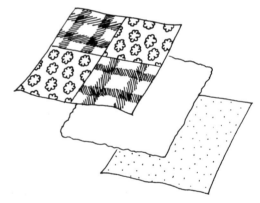

10. Pin the three layers together, then baste them together with rows of long running stitches. Remove pins.

11. Thread the quilting needle with a foot-long piece of thread and knot the end. Begin quilting, following the penciled lines. The quilting stitch is a short running stitch.

Bring the needle from the underside through the three layers to the top.* Take a short running stitch through all three layers. Continue taking short running stitches. Try to keep the stitches as close together as possible, and make the stitches even.

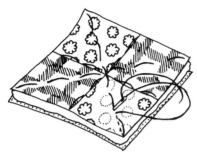

12. Continue quilting, following the pencil lines, until all the quilting is done.†

13. Next, bind the edges with bias tape. To do this, place the patchwork right side up on a flat surface. Fit the bias tape over the edges so that half the tape shows on the front and half shows on the back. Pin the tape in place. Leave a 2-inch-long piece of bias tape at one corner to make a loop. Baste the tape in place and remove pins.

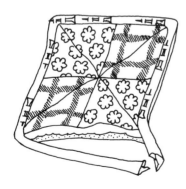

14. Stitch the tape in place with a running stitch. Be sure to catch both edges of the tape.

15. Make a loop of tape in one corner and stitch in place.

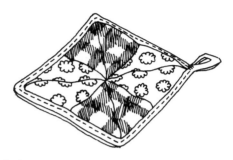

Pointers

There's nothing wrong with leaving the knots showing on the back, but if you want to hide them, pull the thread gently so that the knot is pulled into the batting. When you are out of thread, take several backstitches to secure the thread end.

† It's easier to take several running stitches at once if you hold the work in your lap instead of laying it on a table.

Variations

Make potholders with other patchwork designs. You can also use a single piece of fabric or prequilted fabric. Part of an old towel is another possibility.

3. Jeans Pocket

SKILL

Add a patchwork pocket to your favorite pair of jeans or to a skirt. Or cover a worn spot with a pocket-sized patch. But instead of square patches, try triangles. The pocket is made of eight right triangles in a pinwheel design. Fitted together, they make a square. This pinwheel pattern was one that young pioneer girls liked to sew for their quilts because of its simplicity. The only tricky part is getting the triangles to match perfectly in the center.

The finished pocket is $5\frac{1}{2}$ inches square. You might want to change the size to cover an existing pocket. If so, remember to adjust the other dimensions before you do any cutting.

First you'll cut eight fabric triangles and sew them together for the pocket front. The patchwork is then joined with a piece of filling (or batting) and a piece of fabric backing. The edges of the backing are folded over for the border. Lastly, the pocket is stitched to the garment.

What You Need

Supplies. A pencil, a ruler, scissors, a sheet of tracing paper (optional), glue (optional), a 5-inch-square piece of stiff cardboard, a 5-inch-square piece of heavy paper, pins, a needle, white thread, colored thread for basting, and an iron.

Materials. The pinwheel pattern works with just two alternating fabrics, but this pocket uses four fabrics. You can easily mix solids, stripes, and prints, but when selecting prints, remember that the triangles are small, so a small-scale design will look better than a large-scale design. All the fabrics should be of the same weight.

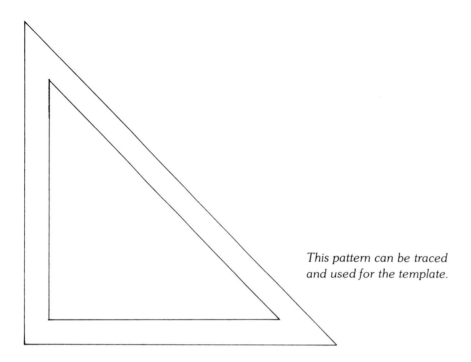

This pattern can be traced and used for the template.

Since you need so little of each fabric, check the remnant tables in stores. You might even use part of an old shirt or handkerchief. If you haven't read them already, look at the sections "Fabric Facts" and "Shopping for Fabric" in the chapter "What You Need."

For the backing, you need a 6¹/₂-inch-square piece of fabric (you can use the same fabric you used for some of the triangles). For the filling you need a 5¹/₂-inch-square piece of quilt batting or flannel.

How to Make

1. Preshrink the fabric by soaking it in warm water. Let it dry, and press it flat.

2. Make a window template using the actual-size pattern given here. Trace the pattern on a sheet of tracing paper. Glue it to a piece of cardboard and cut to size. Or draw a right triangle with 2¹/₂-inch sides directly on cardboard. Add ¹/₄-inch-wide seam allowances and cut the cardboard to size.

3. Place the template on the wrong side of each fabric. Remember that patches should be cut on the straight grain of the fabric. This means that one leg of the triangle is parallel to the selvage. Also, you need two patches of each fabric, so if you want them to look the same, position the template on the same part of the design.

4. Trace the cutting line and the seam line with a pencil.

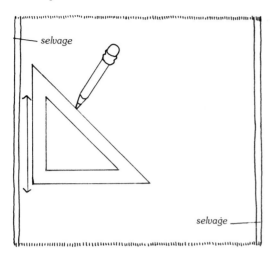

5. Cut out the patches.

6. On a piece of heavy paper, arrange the triangles so that they radiate from the center like a pinwheel (or windmill). When you're satisfied with the patchwork design, pin the patches to the heavy paper. Follow the numbered sketch to sew the patches together.

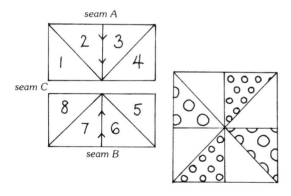

7. Pick up patches 1 and 2. Pin, then baste them together along the hypotenuse, or long side of the triangle, with the right sides of the fabric facing each other. Remove pins and stitch. Trim away any material that extends beyond the corners.

8. Join triangles 3 and 4, 5 and 6, 7 and 8, the same way. Press the seams to one side.

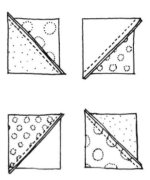

9. Now join the four small squares. Sew seam A. Press. Sew seam B. Press.

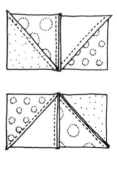

10. Seam C requires careful attention because you want the patches to meet at the center. Insert a pin through the exact center and pin the two sections together from the center out. Take a basting stitch in the center and baste seam C. Remove pins and stitch. Press.

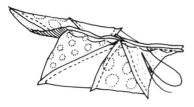

11. Cut a 5 1/2-inch square of quilt batting or flannel. If you use quilt batting, separate it into layers and use the thinnest possible layer. Cut a fabric backing 6 1/2 inches square.

12. Place the backing *right side down* on a flat surface. Center the batting on top, then place the patchwork *right side up* on top of the batting.

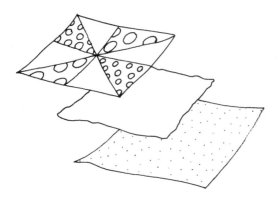

13. Pin, then baste the three layers together lengthwise, crosswise, and diagonally.* Remove the pins.

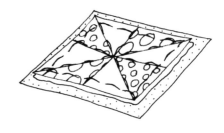

14. The 1/2 inch of backing extending beyond the patchwork becomes the border.† Fold the backing so that its outside edge touches the edge of the patchwork.

Fold again, bringing the backing over and on top of the patchwork.

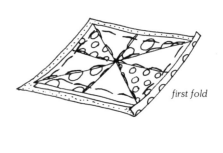

first fold

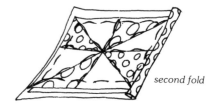

second fold

24

Pin the border in place. At the corners, fold the two strips perpendicular to each other.

15. Slipstitch the border in place. Remove basting.

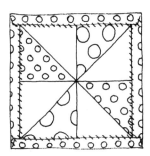

16. To attach the pocket to your pants or skirt, slipstitch it in place, leaving the top seam open. Be sure to take secure stitches. If you plan to carry coins or keys in the pocket, you may want to topstitch it in place or use an embroidery stitch to ensure the pocket's strength.

Pointers

* *Your aim is to make the three layers as smooth and flat as possible, so it's best to pin from the center out, smoothing with one hand while pinning with the other.*
† *The border could also be finished with bias tape as for the Quilted Potholder. If you use this method, make the backing the same size as the patchwork.*

Variation

Pockets are all sizes and shapes, so make one like a crazy quilt. Sew different-sized patches randomly together until you have the size patchwork material you need.

4. String Tote

It looks like a pillow case with a string. It's made of two patchwork panels—and they don't have to match. It's a book bag, a toy bag, a scrap bag, a laundry bag, or a roomy tote to take on an outing. Get into the patchwork spirit. Make a heavyweight bag by recycling old jeans or other worn-out pants for several patches. Remember, use the good parts of the fabric, not the worn parts. Or make a lighter-weight bag using fabric from old shirts or dresses. Collect scraps from relatives and friends who sew. Just make sure that all the fabric is of the same weight—don't mix denim with light-weight cotton, for example. For more information on choosing fabric, see page 2.

The tote is made of two patchwork panels, twelve patches each. First you cut, then you piece the patches for each panel. Unless the bag is a scrap bag, you want the inside to look finished, so the bag is lined. Two lining pieces are cut and stitched together. Then the lining and patchwork are joined. Lastly, the top edges are folded and hemmed to make an inch-wide casing for cord or string.

What You Need

Supplies. A pencil, a ruler, scissors, a 6-inch-square piece of stiff cardboard, two 15-by-20-inch pieces of heavy brown paper, pins, a needle, white thread, colored thread for basting, and an iron.

Materials. The amount of each fabric you need depends on how many different fabrics you are using and the patchwork design. The two panels can be different—one might be made of only two fabrics, and the other of twelve. In all, you need twenty-four patches, each one 6 inches square. The lining material should be light- or medium-weight cotton, and you need about ¾ yard from which to cut two 16-by-21-inch pieces. Buy 2 yards of cord or heavy string for the drawstring.

How to Make

1. Preshrink the fabric by soaking it in warm water. Let it dry, and press.
2. Make a 6-inch-square cardboard template. (The finished patches are 5 inches square, and the seam allowance is ½ inch.)

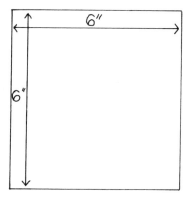

3. Place the template on the wrong side of each fabric and trace it with a pencil. You need twenty-four patches in all.
4. Cut out the fabric patches and mark the ½-inch seam lines.
5. Cut two pieces of heavy brown paper, each 15 by 20 inches. On each piece of paper, arrange patches for a patchwork panel. The panels are each three patches wide by four patches long. The top row of

28

patches won't show full size when the casing is sewn, so don't plan a design where this matters. When you are satisfied with the arrangement of patches, pin them in place on the paper, overlapping them by ½ inch.
6. At last, it's time to sew. Sew one panel at a time. The numbered sketch shows the order for joining the patches.

A	I	2	3
B	4	5	6
C	7	8	9
D	10	11	12

To join the patches, pin two patches, right sides facing, along the seam line. Baste, then remove the pins and stitch. Press all seams to one side.

Join patches 1 and 2, 2 and 3, 4 and 5, 5 and 6, and so on. Be sure to keep all the

seams the same width—½ inch. You now have four strips. Repin them to the brown paper so that you can keep track of them.*

7. Next, join rows A and B, B and C, C and D. The first panel is pieced. Are you tired of sewing? Ask a brother, sister, or best friend to help sew patches for the second panel.

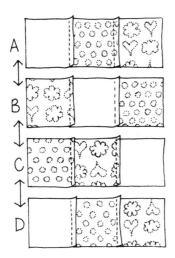

8. Repeat steps 6 and 7 to complete the second panel.

9. On the wrong side of each patchwork panel, draw a line 2½ inches down from the top edge all the way across the panel. This is the casing line.

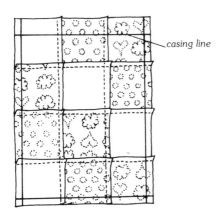

10. With the right sides of the patchwork panels facing, pin, then baste them together. Begin at one end of the casing line and work around three sides, stopping at the other end of the casing line (see the drawing). Leave the top seam open.

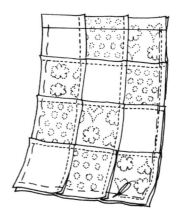

11. Stitch around three sides. Remove the basting.

12. Trim the lower corners on the diagonal to reduce bulk. Press the seams open.

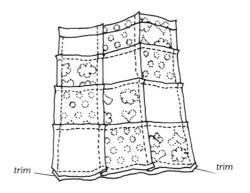

Leave the patchwork with the wrong sides facing out.

13. Next, make the lining. Cut two lining pieces 16 inches wide by 21 inches long. On the wrong side of each piece, mark $1/2$-inch seam lines on the sides and bottom. Draw a line $2^{1}/_{2}$ inches down from the top edge, as you did for the patchwork panels (step 9).

14. With the right sides of the lining facing, pin, then baste around three sides, leaving the top seam open. Begin and end at the casing line, as for the patchwork panels.

15. Stitch the lining. Remove the basting. Press the seams open.

16. Next, attach the lining to the bag. Turn the lining so that the right sides face out. Slip the patchwork inside the lining, matching the seams of the patchwork and lining.

17. Turn the top edges of the lining and patchwork under $1/2$ inch, toward the lining, and baste in place.

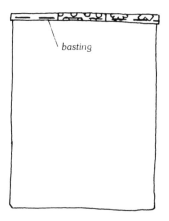

basting

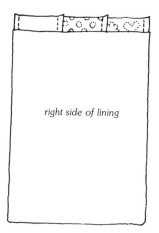

right side of lining

18. Still working on the lining side, make the casing for the cord. Bring the folded edge over 1 inch, and pin in place along the casing line. Baste all the way around the hem. Remove pins.

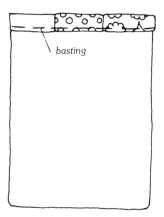

basting

30

19. Hem the casing at the lower edge. Use a straight stitch on the sewing machine, or a running stitch or slipstitch if hand-sewing. Remove the basting.

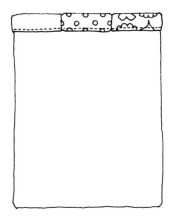

20. Turn the bag right side out.
21. Cut two pieces of cord, approximately 1 yard each. Thread one through the opening in the casing on one side, and out the other side. Thread the other piece through the casing opening opposite the first, and out through the other side.†
22. Knot the loose ends together. Pull the strings. You're ready to tote.

Pointers

* The heavy brown paper is a good way to keep track of patches before they're joined. And by repinning joined patches to the paper, you're sure to join the rows in the proper order. You can also use shelving paper.

† A safety pin is a handy aid in threading the cord through the casing. Attach a safety pin to one end of the cord. Maneuver the pin through the casing with the cord trailing.

Variations

Now that you know how to make a basic tote bag, you can combine this with other projects in this book to make a variety of totes. Make the Jeans Pocket. Then make a tote from a solid-color fabric. Attach the pocket to the outside of the tote. Or appliqué a tote. Cut fabric shapes following the directions for Heavenly Cutouts and stitch them to the outside of a solid-color tote.

5. Squeeze-Me Blocks

SKILL

Squeeze them, stack them, pinch them, hug them. Easy-to-sew patchwork blocks are a delightful present for a younger brother or sister. For each block you need six patches. Use colorful and bold fabrics. For a unique twist, make blocks a touch-me toy as well—with a fuzzy patch, a furry patch, a satiny smooth patch. See how many textures you can combine.

The directions that follow are for one block. For a set of four you need twenty-four patches. Each finished patch is 4 inches square. After cutting out six patches, you'll arrange them right side down in a cross, then sew them together so that you have a fabric box. The box is turned right side out, foam is inserted, and the final patch—the lid—is stitched in place.

What You Need

Supplies. A pencil, a ruler, a 5-inch-square piece of stiff cardboard, scissors, a 12-by-16-inch piece of heavy brown paper, pins, a needle, white thread, colored thread for basting, and an iron.

Materials. This is one project where any soft fabric is suitable. For each block, you need small amounts of six fabrics if each side of the cube is different. Scraps of gingham, corduroy, or felt, and any cotton fabric from another project could be used. For each block, you need a 4-inch cube of foam. Foam can be bought at variety stores and sewing stores. Some stores will cut it to size, but you may have to buy a large piece and carve the blocks yourself. If so, try to find

33

4-inch-thick foam. Then part of the work is already done. Ask an adult for help in cutting it.

How To Make

1. Make a 5-inch-square template from cardboard, or use the actual-size pattern for the Nine-Patch Pillow.
2. Lay the template on the wrong side of each fabric and trace around it with a pencil. You need six patches for each block.
3. Cut out the patches. Mark the seam lines 1/2-inch from each edge.

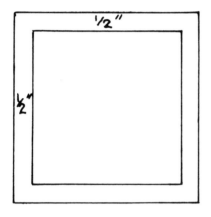

4. Cut out a 12-by-16-inch piece of heavy paper. Arrange the patches in a cross, overlapping them 1/2 inch.*
5. Pin the patches to the paper.
6. You're ready to sew. Follow the numbered sketch. First, join patches 1 and 2. Next, join patches 2 and 3, and patches 3

and 4. Then, join patches 5 and 2, and patches 6 and 2. Press seams to one side.

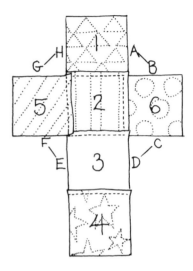

7. The patches will form a cross. Now, still working on the wrong side, join patches 1 and 6 (sides A and B on the sketch). Stitch from the inside corner out.

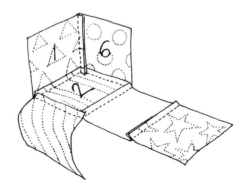

8. Join patches 3 and 6 (sides C and D), patches 3 and 5 (sides E and F), and patches 5 and 1 (sides G and H) the same way. Press seams to one side.

9. Turn the patchwork right side out.

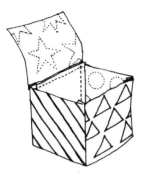

10. Take the 4-inch cube of foam and insert it in the patchwork box. You may have to struggle, because the fabric sticks to the foam.

11. Now, sew the lid on the box—patch 4 is connected to patches 1, 5, and 6. Turn the edges under at the seam lines. Pin, and then baste the remaining seams. Stitch, using a closely spaced whipstitch.†

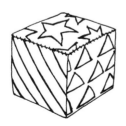

Pointers

* To help determine which patch goes where, temporarily pin the patches to the foam cube so that you can see which patches touch.

† The last patch will be easier to sew in place if you turn the raw edges under at the seam lines and press them. Then insert the cube. The material will stay flat as you sew.

Patchwork Cubes

It's possible to make any size cube following these directions. Make a 24-inch cube and use it as a footrest for your favorite chair. Make 2-inch cubes and hang them on thin rods for an unusual mobile. If you feel ambitious, make a patchwork-game cube. One side can have sixty-four squares for a checkerboard. On another side join nine patches for a tick-tack-toe board. The game cube can be made from felt, lightweight vinyl, or even terry cloth.

6. Mini Quilt

SKILL

A gay, colorful cotton print makes an inviting quilt to cuddle under while watching TV or traveling in a car. You can also make it as a baby quilt. This is not a patchwork project. You will use a single piece of printed fabric for the top and quilt in a design inspired by the fabric. (The quilting directions, though, can also be applied to patchwork.)

Using a single piece of fabric is a quick way to make a quilt. Look for fabric with a large design motif—3-inch-wide butterflies or flowers, for example. Then you can stitch around each object and show off the design. (My fabric had a design of chunks of cheese, and I quilted around each one. This made the cheese stand out.)

A large-scale design is a good choice for another reason: there's less quilting to do.

Hand-quilting is suggested because it's easier for beginners than machine-quilting, but it does take time. I wouldn't recommend machine-quilting unless you're a skilled sewer, because two layers of fabric and a filling are bulky and hard to control.

The finished quilt is 48 inches square.

37

First, you assemble the top, batting, and backing. Then, the three layers are quilted—anchored together with lines of running stitches. Usually the design to be quilted is lightly drawn on the fabric with a pencil, but for this project the outlines of the printed design show where to stitch.

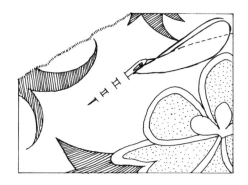

Hand-quilting How-tos

If you examine a beautiful old handmade quilt, you'll be struck by the regularity of the stitches and by how small they are. Traditional quilters aimed for twelve stitches per inch. It's hard to see such small stitches, much less sew them! Luckily for us, using materials available for today's quilters, the size of the stitch isn't so important. Polyester batting doesn't tear and lump the way cotton batting did in great-grandmother's day. Today's quilting is more decorative—the quilt won't fall apart if you make long stitches, though the smaller, the better. The stitches should be even, though, so that the quilt will lie flat.

The quilting stitch is a simple running stitch. Use a #8 or #9 short needle and cotton thread (it won't knot) and take small running stitches through all three layers of fabric. At first, be content to take one stitch at a time. After you've been quilting awhile, you'll be able to take several stitches at once without poking yourself. The stitches should be close together and be all of the same length.

There's no mystery about beginning or ending a line of quilting. Thread the needle with a foot-long piece of thread and tie a knot. Pull the thread from the underside of the backing to the top. Tug gently so that the knot passes through the backing into the batting. If you pull too hard, the knot pops through to the top. If this keeps happening, simply leave the knot showing on the back.

When you're nearly out of thread, stop. Make a knot before the last stitch. Take the stitch but don't go all the way through to the back. Push the needle back through the top as if to take another stitch. The knot should be pulled into the batting. Another way to end is to take several backstitches. Snip the thread and begin where you left off with a new length of thread.

There's no need to use a quilting frame. I find the most comfortable way to work is with the quilt in my lap. I quilt from the center of the work toward my body, which helps me to keep the stitches small and even.

What You Need

Supplies. A yardstick, a pencil, scissors, a ruler, pins, a sewing needle, a quilting needle (#8 or #9), white thread (mercerized cotton or cotton-wrapped polyester if possible), colored thread for basting, and an iron.
Materials. 1¹/₃ yards of 54-inch wide printed fabric for the quilt top (you need a 48-inch-square piece). The fabric should be cotton or a cotton blend, and the design motif to be quilted should be at least 1 inch square. You need a 48-inch-square piece of polyester quilt batting. Batting comes in large rolls, so measure and cut the proper-sized piece and save leftover batting for another project. You need 1¹/₂ yards of 54-inch-wide fabric for the 52-inch-square backing. Backing is usually a solid color, but it doesn't have to be. When buying the fabric for the backing, keep in mind that some of it will show on the top of the quilt as the border.

How To Make

1. Preshrink the fabric by soaking it in warm water. Let it dry, and press if necessary.
2. Measure and cut the fabric for the top, which is 48 inches by 48 inches. Cut the batting the same size. Cut the backing, which is 52 inches by 52 inches. Work on a flat surface such as the floor or a table.*
3. On the wrong side of the backing, lightly pencil a line 2 inches in from each edge. This is a guide for centering the batting and top. It's best to do this with a yardstick.

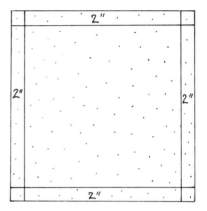

4. Place the backing right side down on the floor. Lay the batting on top of it, using the penciled lines to center the batting. Next, lay the quilt top, right side up, on top of the batting. Check to make sure the batting and top are even with the penciled lines.

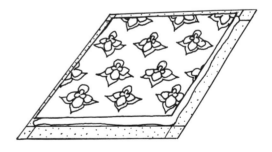

5. Pin all three layers together, starting in the center. Place pins every 2 inches or so,

smoothing and flattening the fabric as you pin outward toward the edges.†

6. Baste the three layers together with long running stitches. Baste horizontally, vertically, and diagonally. Also, baste around the perimeter, about 3 inches from the edge. All this basting keeps the fabric from shifting as you quilt. Remove the pins.

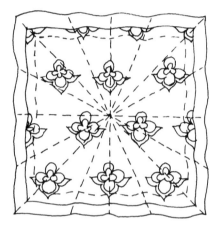

7. You're ready to quilt. Thread the quilting needle with a foot-long length of thread. Start near the center of the quilt and quilt around the chosen design motif. Make short, even running stitches, trying to keep the stitches even. Quilt around each design motif until all the quilting is done.††

8. Next, make the 1-inch-wide border. The backing that shows on each side becomes the border. Fold the edge of the backing in half, turning it toward the top of the quilt. The raw edge of the backing should just touch the raw edge of the quilt top. Bring the folded edge over and on top of the quilt. Pin in place. Make the border folds perpendicular at the corners.

9. Baste the border in place, then remove the pins.

10. Slipstitch the border in place. Remove the basting.

Pointers

* To cut fabric evenly, cut with one hand and hold the fabric flat with the other. Use sharp fabric scissors and make long, even cuts.

† Pinning determines whether the quilt will be flat or lumpy. Space pins close together and use lots of pins. Try to keep them going in the same direction. Check the back to make sure the pins don't make wrinkles in the backing.

†† A thimble is a big help in pushing the needle through all three layers, and it prevents sore fingers. If you hate to wear a thimble, wrap some adhesive tape around your middle finger to protect it. Some quilters find it helpful to roll the quilt up and quilt a section at a time. When one section is finished, roll it up and unroll another.

Variations

This same quilt can be stitched in an all-over quilted design, giving it a more old-fashioned look. This means that instead of quilting around the printed design of the fabric, lines of quilting cover the whole surface. All-over quilting is done by lightly penciling the lines to be quilted on the right side of the quilt top. Then, the three layers are assembled and you quilt following the penciled lines. After quilting, you can erase the penciled lines, but you probably won't have to because they'll be covered by the stitches.

Some easy quilting patterns to try are squares, circles, evenly spaced diagonal lines, and just about any geometric shape you can think of.

For an all-over quilting pattern for a Mini Quilt, try a checkerboard with lines spaced 4 inches apart. This spacing gives the quilt a puffy look. If you want the quilt flatter, space the lines 1 inch apart. Remember to pencil the lines on the right side of the quilt top before basting the three layers together. After quilting, the border is finished as described for the Mini Quilt.

7. Bicycle Rider's Pouch

SKILL

You're off for a bicycle ride. No need to stuff your pockets with carry-alongs. Pack your bike tools, a snack, your keys, and other small objects in a patchwork pouch. Strap the pouch to your waist, with the pockets in back. The deep pockets keep things from falling out.

The pouch measures 15 inches wide by 7¼ inches long. It's made by attaching a three-patch strip of pockets to a backpiece. Then the top edge of the back is folded and hemmed for a casing for the tie. You wear the pouch with the wrong side of the fabric next to your body, so that the colorful pockets show. The finished pockets are each 5 inches square.

First you'll make the three-pocket strip. Then you'll join the pockets and back. Next, the side edges are finished and the top edge is folded and hemmed for a ½-inch-wide casing. It's a good idea to read the directions from start to finish before starting work.

What You Need

Supplies. A pencil, a ruler, scissors, a 6-inch-square piece of stiff cardboard, pins, a needle, white thread, colored thread for basting, and an iron.

Materials. One-quarter of a yard of medium or heavyweight cotton for the back, which is 16 inches by 8½ inches. You'll need three 6-inch-square patches, each of a different fabric, for the pockets. You might recycle some old clothes for this project. Denim, duck, canvas, ticking, and other sturdy fabrics can be used. A long shoelace or a leather thong makes a nice tie.

How to Make

1. Preshrink the fabric by soaking it in warm water. Let it dry, and press it.

2. Measure and cut the back 16 inches wide by 8 1/2 inches high.

3. On the wrong side of the back, mark 1/2-inch seam lines and the 3/4-inch fold line.

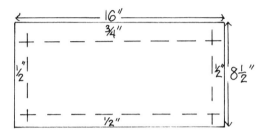

4. Make a 6-inch-square cardboard template for the patch pockets.

5. Outline three patches with the template and cut them out.

6. On the wrong side of each patch, draw lines 1/2 inch from each edge. The side and bottom lines are seam lines; the top line is the fold line.

7. Join the three patches in a row. With right sides facing, pin patches 1 and 2 together along the side seam lines. Baste and remove pins. Stitch. Remove basting. Now stitch patch 3 to patch 2. Press the seams open.

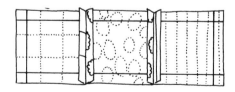

8. Finish the pockets at the top edge by turning the edge 1/4 inch toward the wrong side, then folding it again along the fold line. Pin in place.

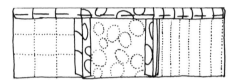

9. Baste the edge with long running stitches.* Then, hem the edge with a running stitch or slipstitch.

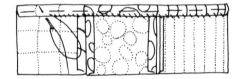

10. Sew the pouch back and the pockets at the lower edge. Position them so that the right side of the pockets faces the wrong side of the back, and match the lower edges (see the drawing). Pin, then baste along the seam line. Remove pins.

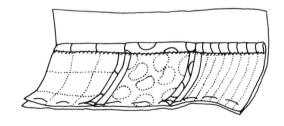

11. Stitch with a running stitch. Remove basting. Press the seam toward the pockets.
12. Turn the pockets so that the right side faces you, and tack them to the back (see the drawing). An easy way to tack is to take a long running stitch in the same place five or six times.

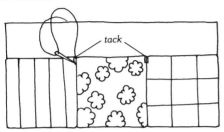

13. The side edges are finished on the wrong side of the pouch where they won't be seen. Fold the front and back side edges 1/4 inch toward the back. Fold again along the fold line. Pin in place; then baste, remove pins, and stitch.†

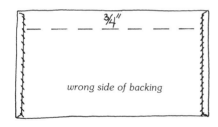

14. Make a casing for the tie by folding the top edge 1/4 inch toward the wrong side. Fold again along the fold line. Pin the 1/2-inch-wide casing in place. Baste, remove pins, and hem the casing. Stitch close to the lower edge.

15. Thread a long shoelace or a leather thong through the casing.

Pointers

A double fold gives the pocket edge a professional look and prevents the fabric from raveling. Make the first fold and press it. Then make the second fold and press. The pressing keeps the raw edge from popping out.
†*The stitching doesn't have to be hidden. If you want it to show, use a running stitch or an embroidery stitch and a contrasting-color thread or embroidery floss.*

Variations

This pouch can also be worn in front as a carpenter's apron. You might want to adjust the dimensions so that the pouch will be large enough to hold long nails and tools.

To personalize a pouch, appliqué your name on it. Appliqué How-tos are given in the directions for Heavenly Cutouts.

8. Workshirt Yoke

SKILL

Dress yourself in patchwork. Brighten up an ordinary workshirt with a patchwork yoke. The yoke can be made to fit any shirt. How? *You* make the pattern. Once you learn how to do this, you'll be busy adding patchwork collars, cuffs, panels, and bands to ready-made clothing.

First, make a paper pattern for a yoke to fit your shirt. Then, make patchwork material. After that, you lay the pattern on the patchwork material and cut out the yoke.

The yoke is a brick design—the patches are of the same height but of different lengths. So here's a chance to experiment with combinations of squares and rectangles. Patches for this yoke are $1^1/_2$ inches square and $1^1/_2$ by $2^1/_2$ inches. The brick design can also be done using patches of only one shape.

Making the Patterns

Directions are for the front and back of a shirt. Since this amounts to quite a lot of sewing, you may want to start with a yoke for only the front or the back.

What You Need

Supplies. A sharp pencil, several sheets of tracing paper, pins, scissors, a piece of cardboard approximately $8^1/_2$ by 11 inches (or large enough to support the shirt yoke), and the shirt to be decorated.

What You Do

1. Study your shirt to determine the exact area the patchwork will cover. Outline the

47

area on the shirt with a pencil. Do not include the button and buttonhole columns. Have the patchwork stop at the edge of these areas (see the drawing).

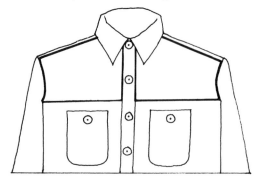

2. For the right front, pin the right-front section of the shirt to a piece of cardboard so that it's flat. The cardboard keeps the shirt from slipping.

3. Lay the shirt with the cardboard inside on a flat surface and place a sheet of tracing paper on top of the right front. (You may need to tape several sheets of tracing paper to make a large enough piece.) Trace the outlined area. Be especially careful at the neckline and armholes to mark the curves accurately. Remember to stop the pattern at the button column. Most shirts have a line of stitching that makes a convenient stopping point.

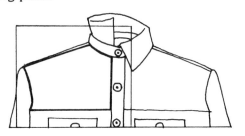

4. Remove the tracing paper and add 1/4-inch-wide seam allowances to the tracing. The outer line is the cutting line.

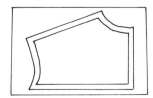

5. Cut out the paper pattern. The same pattern can be used for the left front. It's simply turned right side down. Check to make sure the pattern fits both sides.

6. Unpin the shirt. If you are patchworking the back yoke, pin the back to the cardboard and repeat the tracing process to make the back pattern.

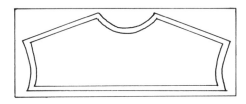

Making the Patchwork

The finished height of each patch is $1\frac{1}{2}$ inches, and the yoke uses a $1\frac{1}{2}$-inch square and a $1\frac{1}{2}$-by-$2\frac{1}{2}$-inch rectangle. You need about twenty patches for each front section and about forty patches for the back, but the exact number depends on your shirt and how you arrange the patches. The plan of the patchwork can be random—it's not necessary to firmly fix a design. Try alternating squares and rectangles, or make one row of squares, then a row of rectangles.

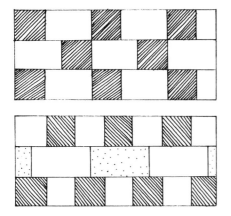

Cut extra patches from each fabric so that you can experiment. This yoke uses four different fabrics, and each section of the front has about five patches of each fabric. But interesting effects can result from just two fabrics, or many different ones. The right- and left-front sections don't have to match, but do use the same fabrics for both.

The first step is to determine the size patchwork material to make. Measure the paper patterns at their widest and longest points. Add 1 inch to each dimension. For example, if the right front measures 9 inches by 7 inches, your patchwork material should be a 10-by-8-inch rectangle. The next step is to cut out the patches and piece them together so that you have a piece of patchwork material the size of the rectangle. Then you will trim the patchwork to fit the paper pattern.

What You Need

Supplies. A pencil, a ruler, a 5-by-4-inch piece of stiff cardboard, scissors, pins, a 15-by-20-inch piece of heavy brown paper, a needle, white thread, colored thread for basting, and an iron.

Materials. For the front and back of the yoke, you need approximately 1/8 yard each of four fabrics. You can use fewer or more fabrics, but the directions are based on four. Remember that all the fabrics should be the same weight, and medium-weight cotton and cotton blends are preferred. Since this project is ideal for using fabric scraps, make sure that any scraps you use have a nice texture and are easy to handle.

How to Make

1. Preshrink the fabric by soaking it in warm water. Let it dry, and press if necessary.
2. Make cardboard templates. The templates include 1/4-inch-wide seam allowances. You need a 2-inch-square template and a 2-by-3-inch rectangle.

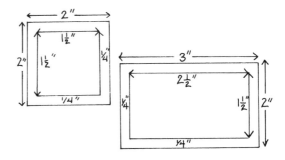

3. If using four fabrics, you need about ten patches of each fabric for the two front sections and about ten of each fabric for the back. You may want both squares and rectangles of each fabric, or all the rectangles of one fabric and all the squares of another. These numbers allow for several extra patches of each fabric. The exact number will depend on your shirt size and your design. To make the patches, place the template on the wrong side of each fabric and outline it with a pencil. Cut out the patches.

4. Pile like patches together and secure them with a pin. This makes it easy to keep track of the patches.

5. If you used a solid template, draw the seam lines ¼ inch from the edge of each patch.

6. Arrange the patches for each section of the yoke in a design. Remember to make a rectangle of fabric for each section.*

7. When you're satisfied with the arrangement, pin the patches to a piece of heavy paper so that you can keep track of them. It's time to sew.

8. Join the patches in rows. Place two patches with right sides facing. Pin, then baste along the seam line. Remove pins and stitch. If you are hand-sewing, be sure to take small running stitches and sew secure seams. Press the seams to one side.

9. The numbered sketch is a useful guide for joining patches. First, join patches in horizontal strips. Join patches 1 and 2, 2 and 3, 3 and 4, and 4 and 5. Repeat for each row

until you have four strips. Now join rows A and B, B and C, and C and D. Press all the seams to one side.

A	1	2	3	4	5	6
B	7	8	9	10	11	12
C	13	14	15	16	17	18
D	19	20	21	22	23	24

10. Continue joining patches until you complete the patchwork fabric for each section of the yoke. Press the patchwork.

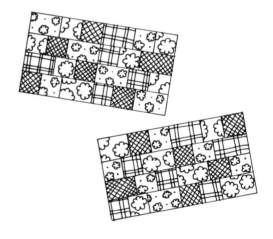

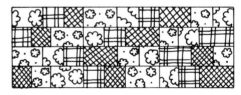

50

11. Now the paper patterns are placed on the patchwork material, and it is trimmed to size. Place the right-front pattern face up on the right side of the patchwork. The bottom of the pattern piece should be in line with the bottom of the patchwork. Pin the pattern in place.

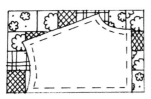

12. Outline the pattern with a sharp pencil. Remove the paper pattern and cut the patchwork following the pencil lines.

13. Make the left front the same way, but remember to place the pattern *right side down* on the patchwork.

14. Trim the patchwork fabric for the back yoke the same way.

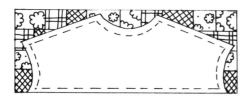

15. Press the patchwork flat. If it looks as though the edges will ravel, sew lines of stay stitching 1/8 inch from the outer edges.†

16. Turn the edges of the patchwork pieces under 1/4 inch. Baste and press. The turned-under edges may be bulky, so clip the curves at the neckline and armholes. Do this by several tiny, spaced cuts where the fabric

bulges (see the drawing). Do not cut right up to the folded edge.

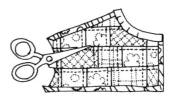

17. Pin, then baste each patchwork section in place on the shirt.

18. Slipstitch in place with tiny stitches. If sewing by machine, topstitch in place.

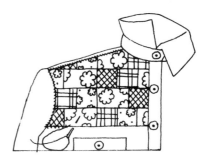

Pointers

* When designing the patchwork, work from the center out. Don't worry about evening up all the rows because you are working with an irregularly-shaped pattern. It's a good idea to lay the patchwork on top of the shirt so you can see where the patches will fall when the yoke is complete.

†Stay stitching is a line of running stitches done on the right side of the work. It prevents edges from raveling and helps the fabric keep its shape.

9. Heavenly Cutouts

This heavenly work of art combines two quilting techniques: appliqué and quilting. The sun and clouds are appliqués, while the sun's rays are double lines of quilting. The finished work is 13 inches by 18 inches. With loops attached, it's an attractive wall hanging. It can also be finished as a pillow.

Appliqué usually means sewing small shapes onto a larger piece of fabric. A paper pattern is drawn for each shape, then a 1/4-inch seam allowance is added. The pattern is cut out and laid on the fabric and traced. Then the fabric shape is cut out, the seam allowance is turned under, and the shape is stitched to the background fabric.

For this project, the fabric sun and clouds are basted and then stitched to a background fabric. The picture is then joined with a layer of filling and a backing fabric. The sun's rays are quilted, and lastly, the raw edges of the work are finished with bias tape.

Heavenly Cutouts shows you several appliqué possibilities, but there are thousands more. After doing this project, you have the necessary skills to appliqué anything. You can design your own appliqués or use shapes you see around you. Interesting shapes are everywhere—books, magazines, wrapping paper, and food packages are excellent sources for beginning ideas.

Appliqué How-tos

The best fabrics for appliqué are soft cottons because they're easy to hem. (Felt is great because it needs no hem at all, but it isn't washable, so don't use it on things you plan to wash.) For this project, the shapes are deliberately simple, so that any fabric is suitable. You might use fabric with a pile for the clouds and a lustrous velvet for the sun. The background fabric should be soft yet sturdy.

The sun and clouds have a turn-under allowance of ¼ inch. It's a good idea to turn the edges under and baste them. Then, when the shape is stitched to the background fabric, the edges won't keep popping out. The most usual appliqué stitch is a blind stitch. Embroidery stitches can also be used if you want added texture. If you have a zigzag sewing machine, try a close zigzag stitch or satin stitch that catches the edges of the appliqué and the background fabric.

Making Paper Patterns

Supplies. Several sheets of tracing paper or notebook paper, a pencil, a compass or string, a ruler, and scissors.

How to Make

1. For the sun, draw a semicircle with a 6½-inch radius. The lower edge of the paper

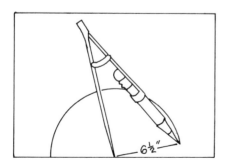

will be the diameter of the circle. If you don't have a compass, fashion one by attaching a 6½-inch-long piece of string to a pencil. Hold the string at the center of the semicircle and move the pencil 180 degrees.

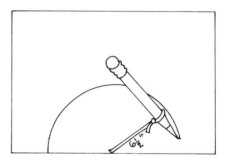

2. Draw a line parallel to the diameter, ¼ inch above it. This is the cutting line.

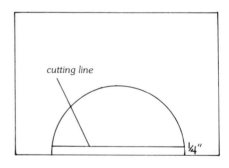

cutting line

¼"

3. Cut out the sun along the cutting line. This pattern includes the ¼-inch turn-under allowance.

4. Draw two clouds freehand on paper. The ones shown here are 6 inches wide by

54

3 inches high. Add ¼ inch for the turn-under allowance. Cut out the paper clouds.

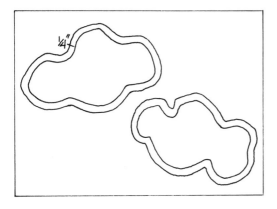

Making the Fabric Picture

Supplies. A pencil, a ruler, scissors, pins, a sewing needle, a quilting needle (#8 or #9 short needle), white thread, colored thread for basting and quilting, scissors, and an iron.

Materials. A 13-by-18-inch piece of medium-weight cotton fabric for the background, a piece of fabric of the same size for the backing (the backing won't show, so you can use part of a bed sheet or some unbleached muslin), and a same-sized piece of polyester quilt batting for filling. You need small amounts of fabric for the sun and clouds. (Fabric for the sun and clouds can be anything, just so long as it's soft.)

For binding the edges, you need a package of 1-inch-wide bias tape. This is pre-folded sewing tape that comes in all colors. If the picture will be hung, you need an 18-inch-long wooden dowel. Dowels are sold at hardware stores or lumberyards.

How to Make

1. Measure and cut the background, batting, and backing. Each one should be 13 by 18 inches. Press the background and backing to remove any wrinkles.
2. Make the sun and cloud appliqués. For each appliqué, take the paper pattern and place it right side up on the *right side* of the fabric. Pin in place. Trace the pattern, then cut out the fabric shape along the tracing lines.
3. Turn the edges of the appliqués under ¼ inch and pin. On the turned-under edges, clip curves by making tiny cuts in the fabric nearly up to, but not all the way to, the fold. The slits should be slightly less than ¼ inch long.

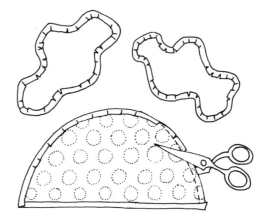

4. Overlap the turned edges of the sun at the corners so that they lie flat (see the drawing). Baste the turned edges in place.*

Space the rays at least an inch apart. (The pencil lines will be covered by the quilting stitches, but keep them as light as you can.)

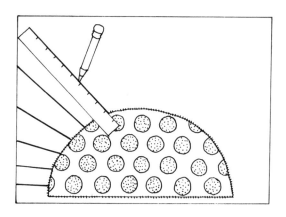

5. Position the sun in the center of the background fabric, 1/4 inch from the lower edge. Baste in place. Sew the sun to the background with a blind stitch.† Remove basting.

7. Pin, then baste the top, batting, and backing together so that they won't shift when you quilt. Baste with thread of a contrasting color, so it will be easier to see and take out when you are finished. Remove pins.

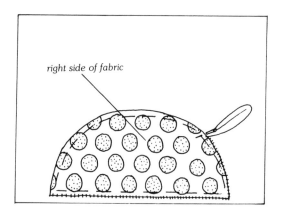

right side of fabric

6. Lightly pencil the sun's rays on the background as if radiating from the sun's center.

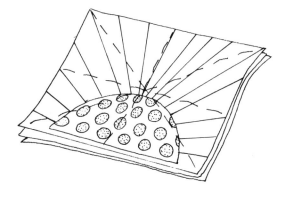

8. Quilt the rays (see the directions for the Mini Quilt for quilting how-tos). Each ray is two parallel lines of running stitches. The two lines should be as close together as possible. Rays can be done with colored or white thread. This depends on your fabric. You want the rays to stand out.

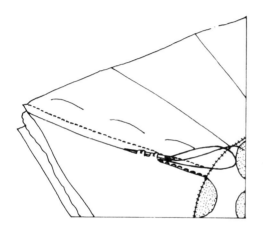

9. Baste the clouds in place. Sew with a blind stitch. Remove basting.

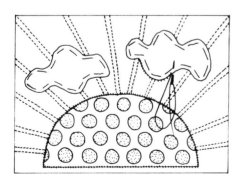

10. Finish the edges with bias tape.†† Cut two 19-inch-long pieces and two 14-inch-long pieces. Place the work right side up on a flat surface. With right sides facing, pin the bias strips so that the raw edges match as shown in the drawing. Sew each strip 1/4 inch from the edge with running stitches. Leave unsewn the 1/2 inch of bias tape that extends beyond each corner.

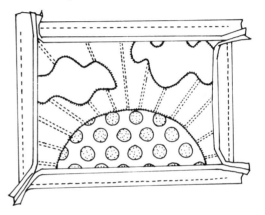

11. Open out the border strips. To miter the corners, turn the work so that the wrong side faces you.

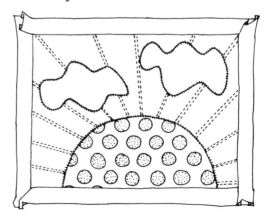

12. At each corner, place the right sides of the bias strips together and secure with a pin. Stitch at a 45-degree angle.

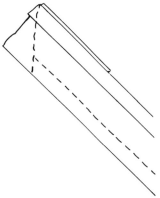

13. Fold the border to the back. Now $1/4$ inch of the border shows on the back and $1/4$ inch shows on the front. Slipstitch in place.

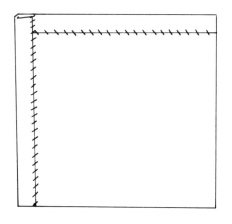

14. For the tabs, cut four 2-inch-long pieces of bias tape. Fold each piece and stitch the ends, making a loop. Sew the tabs to the back, close to the top edge.

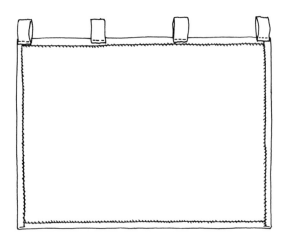

15. To hang, insert a wooden dowel through the loops.

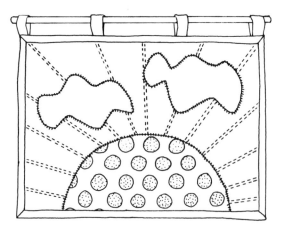

Variation

To finish as a pillow, complete steps 1 through 9. Then cut a piece of fabric 13 by 18 inches for the pillow back. With right sides facing, stitch around three sides, ¼ inch from the edges. Turn the work right side out. Stuff with polyester pillow stuffing. Slipstitch the remaining seam closed.

Fabric Artistry

Any material that can be stitched to fabric can be used for future appliqué projects, so start collecting scraps of leather, lace, felt, ribbon, yarn, and even buttons and feathers. Design a fabric picture using as many materials as possible. Or decorate ready-made clothing with appliqué pictures.

Pointers

Basting keeps the folded edge from popping out. (Edges that ravel badly can be stay-stitched.) Don't press the edges, because the slight puffiness of the fold adds interest.

† All the hemming and basting may seem unnecessary, but it makes sewing the sun in place a breeze. All you have to concentrate on is artful stitching.

†† Instead of bias tape, you might want to use wide ribbon or blanket binding.

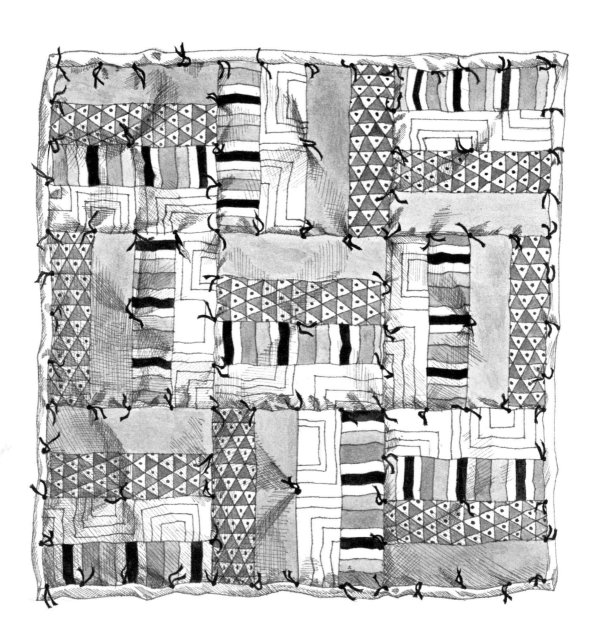

10. Superstripes Quilt

SKILL

This dramatic quilt is a four-patch design that makes an eye-catching bedcover for a single bed or a striking wall hanging. The quilt is made of nine blocks, each consisting of four bands of fabric. Each block is 20 inches square. When you position the blocks horizontally and then vertically, the quilt has a supergraphic look.

Superstripes is tufted—tied with knots of thread—to hold the three layers together. The finished quilt is 60 inches square and looks best on a bed with a dust ruffle covering the frame. If you want to make a bedspread or have the quilt fit another size bed, you must adjust the dimensions of each block and patch. Read the information on quilt sizes, given later in the book, before making changes.

The block method of quiltmaking is a convenient way to work. If you are hand-sewing, you can carry patches for a block with you and piece the block when you have free time. Another advantage is that a quilt can be made larger or smaller simply by adding or subtracting blocks. A block can be any size. Traditional patchwork blocks were usually 12 inches square. Superstripes blocks are purposely large—each one is 20 inches square—so that there are fewer seams to sew.

If you've already tried some of the easier patchwork projects, you're familiar with all the techniques needed to make a quilt. The only difference here is that there's more piecing to do. So, take your time. Don't attempt to finish Superstripes in a week. After all, you'll snuggle under this quilt for years to come.

A Note about Design

Superstripes uses four fabrics, and each block has one stripe of each fabric. Even if you follow this four-fabric design, your quilt will be one-of-a-kind because you'll use different fabrics. You could also use only two fabrics, alternating a dark fabric and a light one. This quilt is very striking done in black-and-white or red-and-white. If you have a storehouse of fabric from other sewing projects, you might consider making each block different. If you change the design, think the project through and carefully plan the number of patches of each fabric before you start to cut.

Many people like to work out designs on graph paper first. Use colored pencils or markers and draw the quilt to scale. Planning the design first is a way to avoid expensive mistakes. You won't find out that you hate pink next to green *after* cutting the fabric.

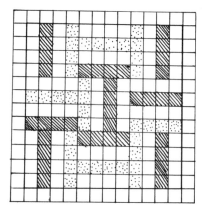

The steps necessary to make this quilt are similar to those described in previous projects. First you'll make a cardboard template, outline the stripes on the fabric, and cut them out. Then you'll sew the four stripes together that make up each block. Next, the blocks are joined to complete the top. The top, batting, and backing are basted together, and the raw edges are finished for the 1-inch-wide border. Lastly, the quilt is tufted to keep the three layers from shifting.

What You Need

Supplies. A pencil, a yardstick, a ruler, a 6-by-21-inch piece of stiff cardboard or posterboard for the template (you may need to tape several sheets to make one large enough), scissors, a 60-by-60-inch piece of heavy brown paper or an old sheet, tape, pins, a needle, white thread, colored thread for basting, and an iron.

Materials. If you use four fabrics for the quilt top, you need approximately 1½ yards of each fabric. Cotton and cotton blends work best. It's better to have extra fabric than to find yourself short. For the 62-by-62-inch backing, you need about 4 yards of fabric. Most fabrics are not wide enough to allow the backing to be made in one piece. You can simply sew two wide strips of fabric together. You will be left with extra fabric, but you can use some of it for the front of the quilt or for another patchwork project.

Or the backing can also be made of un-bleached muslin or a queen-size sheet, both of which are wide enough.

For the filling, you need a 60-by-60-inch, sheet of polyester quilt batting, so buy a large roll. For tufting, you can use crochet thread, buttonhole twist, or embroidery floss.

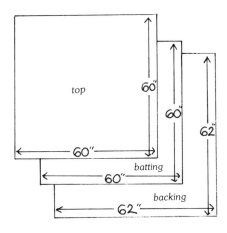

How to Make

1. Preshrink the fabric by soaking it in warm water—the bathtub is a good place to do this. Let it dry, and press if necessary.
2. Make a 6-inch-by-21-inch template (see "How-tos for All Projects" in the front of the

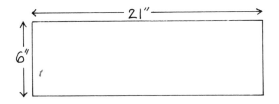

book). Unless you have a large sheet of cardboard, you're better off buying some posterboard, which comes in big sheets. Then you can make the template all in one piece.
3. Lay the template on the wrong side of each fabric and trace it with a pencil. You need thirty-six stripes in all.* If at any time you find that the template edges wear down and are not sharp, make another template for the rest of the stripes. It's important that all the stripes be the same size.
4. Cut out the fabric stripes.
5. Mark the seam lines. The seam allowance is ½ inch.

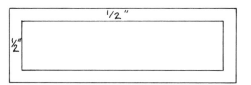

6. Now tape sheets of heavy brown paper together until you have a 60-inch-square piece. If you planned a design on graph paper or are following the design shown here, this is not really necessary, but the brown-paper method is a good way to work. When you pin the patches to the brown paper, you can see what the finished quilt will look like and change the design if necessary. Also, the patches won't get lost or out of order, and you can keep track of them easily by repinning them to the paper

after stitching. The project can be folded and stored out of the way when you're not working on it. An alternative to the brown paper is an old sheet.

7. Arrange the stripes on the brown paper, overlapping them ½ inch. Each block has four stripes, and there are nine blocks in all. The blocks are alternated so that a horizontal block is next to a vertical one, and so on (see the drawing). When you finish arranging the stripes, stand back and admire your work. Pin each stripe to the heavy paper.

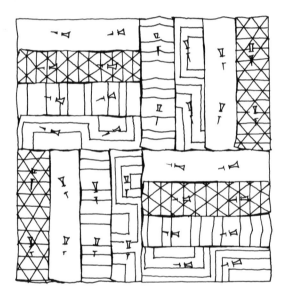

8. Piece one block at a time. The four stripes that make up each block are joined as for any patchwork project. Pick up two adjacent stripes. With right sides facing, pin them together along the seam line. Baste,

then remove pins. Stitch. Press the seams to one side. Repeat until the block is pieced.

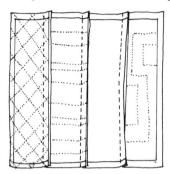

9. Piece all nine blocks, press the seams, and repin them to the brown paper.

10. Next, the blocks are joined in rows. Join blocks 1 and 2 and 2 and 3 in a row. Press the seams to one side. Do the same for blocks 4, 5, and 6, and for blocks 7, 8, and 9. You now have three 60-inch-wide rows.

11. To complete the quilt top, join rows A and B. Join rows B and C. Press seams to one side. Congratulations, the top is done!

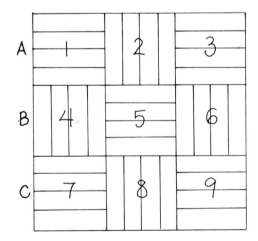

12. Make the backing 62 inches by 62 inches. You probably will have to sew two or more strips of fabric together in order to get a piece this size. If possible, have the seam fall in the center.

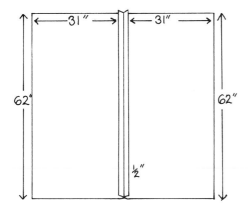

13. On the wrong side of the backing, lightly pencil a line 2 inches in from each edge. This is a guide for centering the batting and patchwork top.

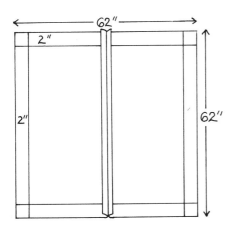

14. Cut the batting 60 inches by 60 inches if you haven't already done so.

15. Lay the backing right side down on the floor. Center the batting on top, the edges even with the pencil lines. Lay the patchwork right side up on top of the batting.

16. Pin the three layers together, starting at the center. Smooth as you pin so that there are no wrinkles in the backing or patchwork.†

17. Baste through all three thicknesses. Start at the center and baste toward the sides in a sunburst. Also, baste around the perimeter, 2 inches from the edge of the top. Remove pins.

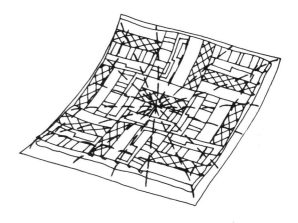

18. Make the border. Fold the backing so that the edge of the backing touches the edge of the patchwork.

Fold it again, bringing the fold on top of the patchwork. Pin in place.††

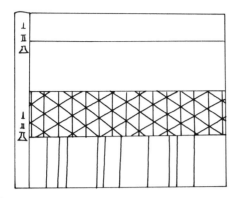

Take another stitch in the same place.

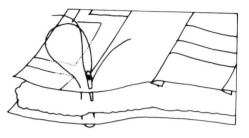

Pull the needle away, leaving two thread ends on top of the quilt. Tie a square knot (right over left, left over right). Trim the thread ends close to the knot.§

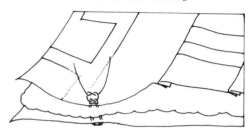

19. At the corners, fold the material so that the folded border edges are perpendicular. Pin, then baste the border in place.

20. Slipstitch the border in place. Remove pins and basting.

21. Tufting holds the three layers together so the quilt won't look lumpy after washing. Use a needle and strong thread, embroidery floss, or crochet thread. Thread the needle with an 8-inch-long piece of thread. Do not knot the thread. Pass the needle through the three layers from front to back. Bring the thread back to the front close to where you began, leaving 2 inches of thread on the quilt top (see the drawings, which for clarity show the quilt without the border in place).

22. Space the tufting as shown in the drawing. If you want to tuft in another pattern, make sure you space the tufts close enough together.

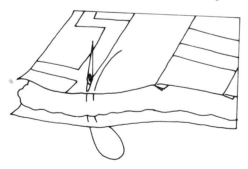

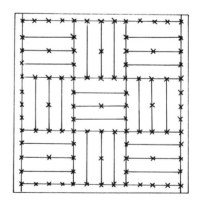

Pointers

When you have many stripes to cut, you can save time by folding the fabric and cutting two or more stripes at a time. But don't try to cut too many at once, because the fabric will shift and the stripes won't be equal. Make sure that your cutting is accurate.

† If all the pins go in the same direction, they're easier to remove and you won't prick yourself.

†† An alternative to the border way of finishing the edges is to have no border showing. The batting and backing are cut the same size as the quilt top, and the raw edges are turned under ¼ inch and hemmed.

§ Practice tufting with three layers of fabric scraps. Check to see that the needle doesn't make a large hole in the fabric. If it does, switch to a needle with a smaller eye.

for the Nine-Patch Pillow. You might even use ribbon for the stripes instead of fabric.

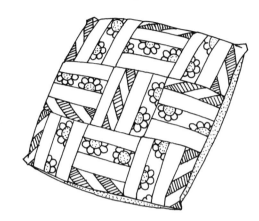

Variations

Superstripes can be quilted instead of tufted. See the directions for the Mini Quilt for quilting how-tos.

This striped design also looks great as a pillow, tote bag, beach bag, or table napkin. To adapt the design, figure the size of the finished object and the size of each stripe. For example, for a 12-inch-square pillow, each finished stripe is 1 inch by 4 inches. Assemble the pillow following the directions

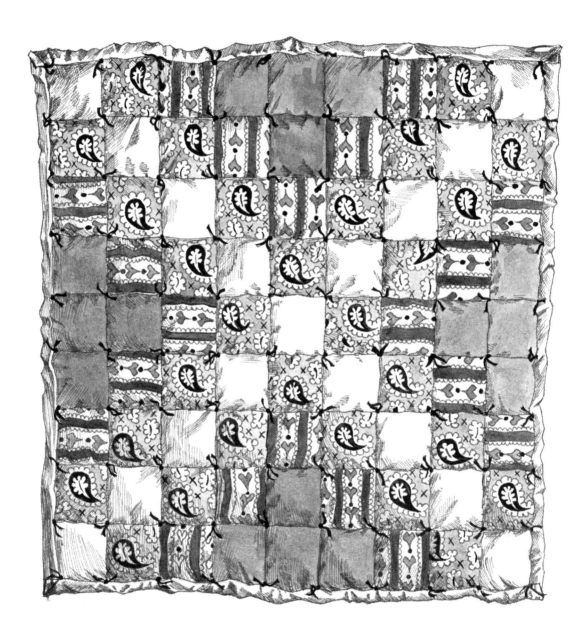

11. Crosschecks Quilt

SKILL

This is a one-patch quilt. Historically, European quilts used the one-patch method, while Americans favored the block-by-block quilting explained for Superstripes (see preceding project). For a one-patch quilt, squares of the same size are simply pieced together into one big block. They can be sewn in a random selection, or a design can be made by beginning at the center and placing patches this way and that to create a geometric design. This quilt design resembles a crossword-puzzle grid.

As with other projects in this book, you needn't follow this exact design. You might try grouping dark patches around a light center, or light patches around a dark center. Or, the design can be random, making use of interesting fabrics you have on hand. By now, you are an experienced quilter, so the directions are abbreviated. If you aren't

quite sure of a step, refer to the directions for Superstripes.

Crosschecks is 63 inches by 63 inches, so it fits a single bed as a coverlet. A coverlet extends to the top of the bed frame, not to the floor. The quilt can be made larger or smaller by adjusting the size of each patch or the number of patches. (For more information, read the section on quilt sizes on page 77.) Each patch is 7 inches square, so you need 81 patches.

What You Need

Supplies. A pencil, an 8-inch-square piece of cardboard, a ruler, scissors, pins, a 63-by-63-inch piece of heavy brown paper (or an old sheet), tape, a needle, white thread, colored thread for basting, and an iron.
Materials. Medium-weight cotton and cotton

blends are suggested. If the fabric is 45 inches wide, you need 1 yard each of three fabrics and 1¼ yards of the fourth fabric. These amounts include extra fabric. For this design you need seventeen patches of fabric A, twenty-eight patches of fabric B, twenty patches of fabric C, and sixteen patches of fabric D.

The back is 65 inches by 65 inches. You need about 4 yards of fabric if the seam is to fall in the center of the backing. The backing might be a sheet or muslin. The filling is a 63-by-63-inch piece of polyester quilt batting.

How to Make

1. Preshrink the fabric.
2. Make an 8-inch-square cardboard template. (Finished patches are 7 inches square, and the seam allowance is ½ inch.)
3. Lay the template on the wrong side of each fabric and outline the patches. If following the design shown here, you need sixteen patches of one fabric, seventeen of another, twenty of another, and twenty-eight of another.
4. Cut out the patches. Draw seam lines ½ inch from the edges if you haven't already done so.
5. Pile like patches together and secure with a pin.
6. Tape heavy paper together until you have a piece 63 inches square.
7. Arrange patches on the heavy paper,

working from the center out, until you have a design you like. Pin each patch to the paper, overlapping by ½ inch.
8. Join all the patches in row A. Press the seams to one side. Repeat for each row until the patches in all nine horizontal rows are joined.

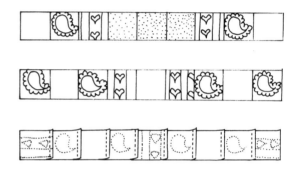

9. Now join rows A through I. Press all the seams to one side. The quilt top is finished.

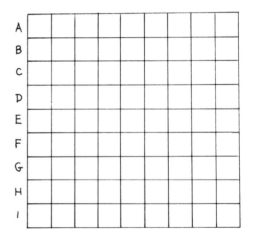

10. Cut the batting the same size as the top.
11. Make a 65-by-65-inch backing. This allows for a 1-inch-wide border.
12. Assemble the three layers of the quilt and pin and baste them together.
13. Complete the border, slipstitching it in place.
14. Tuft, either in the center of each patch or at the joints connecting two patches.

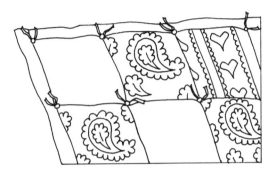

12. Friendship Quilts

SKILL

Follow an old quilting custom and have fun at the same time—make a friendship quilt. In pioneer days, friends got together to make quilts for such special occasions as a wedding or when a family moved west. Each person made a block of the quilt, and then a quilting party was held to sew all the blocks together and quilt the pieced work.

Your family, class, or group of friends can make a Friendship Quilt as a gift or just for your own enjoyment. The quilt doesn't have to be large; it can be a wall hanging instead of a bedcover if you like. A highly individual project is an appliqué quilt where each quiltmaker appliqués a block. Then all the blocks are sewn together. All the quiltmakers might sign their names on their blocks (be sure to use a permanent ink marker).

The first step is to decide on the finished size and the size of each block. This depends on how many people are contributing. A 60-inch-square quilt like Superstripes, for example, has nine 20-inch-square blocks. It could also be done with twenty-five blocks, each 12 inches square. It's also helpful to pick a color scheme so that the finished quilt has unity. Once these decisions are made, it's time to get busy. Here are some suggested themes for appliqué quilts:

Autograph Quilt. Each block represents its maker. Appliqué your name, a fabric drawing of yourself, or a symbol of your hobbies or talents.

It Says You. Each block tells something about the person who will receive the quilt.

Creative Creatures. Each block shows an appliquéd animal. Animals can be fanciful or realistic-looking.

Kitchen Quilt. Favorite foods appear on

each block. If you're really dedicated, stitch your favorite recipe, using embroidery thread.

Sports World. Each block shows a different sport and its players.

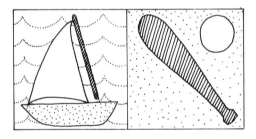

Dream Quilt. Each block expresses a fantasy or dream.

History in the Making. Show the place you like best in your city or town.

The directions for assembling a Friendship Quilt closely follow the directions for the Superstripes Quilt. Consult them for more detailed instructions if you aren't sure of a step.

How to Make

1. Preshrink the fabric.
2. Cut a background fabric for each block. Remember to add ½ inch on all sides for the seam allowance. So, if each block is 20 inches square, the background fabric is 21 inches square.
3. Each person appliqués a block according to the group plan. Appliqué how-tos are explained for Heavenly Cutouts.
4. Arrange all the finished blocks in order, and sew all the blocks together for the quilt top.
5. Press the seams to one side.
6. Cut a backing 2 inches larger than the quilt top all around.
7. Cut a layer of quilt batting the same size as the top.
8. Baste the top, batting, and backing together.
9. Make the border by folding the overlapping backing in half, then bringing the fold on top of the quilt top. Slipstitch in place.
10. Tuft between each block to anchor the three layers.

Moving On

Now that you know the basics of quilting and are a skilled sewer, you can create toys, clothes, bedcovers, and quilted items that are useful and decorative. You can also repeat the projects in this book, trying new patchwork designs and combining techniques. Make the String Tote, for example, quilting a design within each square. Or work out your initials in patchwork and appliqué a Jeans Pocket. Here are some ideas for projects to ponder:

patchwork book cover
patchwork butcher-style apron
stuffed patchwork turtle
appliqué tennis racquet cover
terry patchwork baby bib
patchwork backpack
felt or ribbon patchwork belt
appliqué eyeglass case
quilted chair cushion

. . . And just about anything else you can sew.

QUILT SIZES—FOR QUILTS YOU DESIGN YOURSELF

There's no hard-and-fast rule for the size of a quilt. It depends on the size of the bed and how the quilt will be used. Superstripes and Crosschecks fit a single bed as a coverlet— they reach the top of the dust ruffle on three sides but don't cover the pillows. The best way to determine the size quilt to make is to measure your bed. You need to know the size of the mattress and the drop. The drop is the part of the quilt that hangs over the sides and foot of the bed. For a bedspread, the quilt usually extends to the floor and covers the pillows.

These are the standard mattress sizes:

single (twin) bed	39 by 75 inches
double bed	54 by 75 inches
queen-size bed	60 by 78 inches
king-size bed	72 by 84 inches

Measure the mattress from head to foot and from side to side. Measure the drop— from the top of the mattress to the bed frame or dust ruffle (or to the floor if a bedspread). Add the drop to the mattress measurements. (If you don't want the quilt to reach all the way to the head of the bed, don't add the drop to the length.) If the quilt is to cover the pillow, add 8 inches to the length.

An easier way to figure the size of a quilt is to drape a sheet over the bed. Pin it to fit as a quilt. Then measure the sheet.

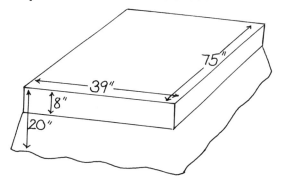

METRIC CONVERSIONS

¼ in. = 6.4 mm = .64 cm
½ in. = 12.7 mm = 1.3 cm
¾ in. = 19 mm = 1.9 cm
1 in. = 25.4 mm = 2.5 cm
1 ft. = 30.5 cm = .30 m
1 yd = 91.4 cm = .91 m
mm = millimeters
cm = centimeters
m = meters

TERMS TO KNOW

When you first learn a new craft, you come across strange words and even some familiar words used in new ways. It's easy to sort out quilting words if you think of a quilt or other quilted object as a sandwich. This means it has three layers: a top, a bottom, and a filling. In quilting, the top—not the filling—gets most of your attention. The top can be patchwork, appliqué, or just a plain piece of material. The top is made first; then the three layers are assembled. To hold the layers together, a quilt is tufted or quilted.

Appliqué

To attach one piece of fabric to a background piece. This differs from patchwork, where shapes are sewn together to make a larger piece of fabric. Appliqué can be used in patchwork.

Backing

The underside or bottom layer of a quilt or quilted object. Usually, the backing is a whole piece of fabric.

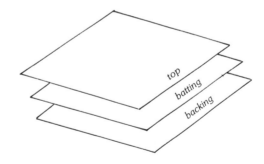

Basting

Large running stitches that temporarily hold fabric in place until the final stitching is done.

Batting

A quilt's middle layer or filling. Batting is usually polyester and looks like white cotton candy. Batting provides warmth and gives body to a quilt.

Binding

Finishing a quilt's edges. One way is to turn the backing over the top and stitch. Another is to add strips of fabric or bias tape around the perimeter to cover the edges.

Block

A section of a quilt. It can be made of only one patch or of many patches.

Border

The edge of the quilt that frames the top.

Coverlet

A bedcover that is large enough to cover the bed but is not used as a bedspread.

Friendship Quilt

A quilt made up of blocks contributed by different people. In pioneer days, neighbors made friendship quilts for happy events, such as a family moving west or a wedding.

Hemming

Turning under an edge and securing it with stitches.

Miter

To join two pieces of fabric at a corner so that they form a 45-degree angle.

Patch

A geometric shape such as a square, triangle, or rectangle, cut from fabric.

Patchwork

Sewing fabric patches together in a design.

Piece

To sew fabric patches together. Patchwork is also called "pieced" work.

Preshrink

To wash fabric in warm water so that it shrinks. This first washing prevents the patchwork from puckering in later washings.

Quilt

A bedcover made of three layers: a top and bottom, with batting or filler in between. The quilt top can be a single piece of fabric, or it can be patchwork.

Quilting

Joining the three layers together with stitches that form a design. Quilting keeps the fabric from shifting. It can be done by hand or with a sewing machine.

Right Side of Fabirc

This is the good side, the side that you want to show.

Seam

To join two pieces of fabric at a common edge.

Seam Allowance
The size of the seam. For most projects, it is ½-inch wide. This means that the seam is sewn ½ inch from the fabric edge.

Seam Line
The line indicating where two pieces of cloth are sewn together.

Selvage
The narrow woven border on the lengthwise edge of fabric.

Straight Grain
The lengthwise threads of the fabric that run parallel to the selvage.

Template
A pattern made of cardboard that's used to outline patches on fabric.

Throw
A small-sized bedcover.

Tufting
Spaced knots of thread or yarn that hold the three layers together. This is also called tying. Patchwork is usually tufted instead of quilted.

Wrong Side of Fabric
The bad side, the side that you don't want to show.

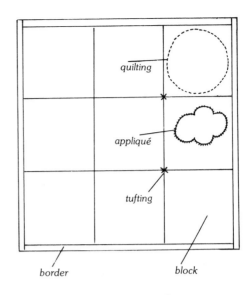

quilting

appliqué

tufting

border

block

INDEX

ABOUT THE AUTHOR

Marilyn Ratner is a children's book writer and editor with a wide-ranging interest in crafts. It took her six months, working day and night, to make her first quilt, an experience that inspired her to design for *Plenty of Patches* projects that beginners could quickly complete!

A graduate of Syracuse University, Marilyn Ratner lives in Scarsdale, New York, with her husband, Michael, and young son, David. She is coauthor of *Many Hands Cooking*, an international children's cookbook (published by T. Y. Crowell in cooperation with the U.S. Committee for UNICEF). She is currently teaching children's cooking classes and doing free-lance writing.

ABOUT THE ILLUSTRATOR

Chris Conover was born and brought up in New York City, where she attended the High School of Music and Art. She has illustrated a number of distinguished books for children, including *The Wish at the Top* by Clyde Robert Bulla and a picture book, *Six Little Ducks*, for which she received a Boston Globe-Horn Book Award. Ms. Conover lives in Brooklyn, New York.